SHROPSHIRE

by

SHIRLEY TART

COUNTRYSIDE BOOKS

NEWBURY · BERKSHIRE

First published 2000
© Shirley Tart 2000

COUNTRYSIDE BOOKS
3 Catherine Road
Newbury, Berkshire

To view our complete range of books,
please visit us at
www.countrysidebooks.co.uk

ISBN 1 85306 639 7

Cover illustration by Louis Mackay
Produced through MRM Associates Ltd., Reading
Typeset by Techniset Typesetters, Merseyside
Printed by Woolnough Bookbinding Ltd., Irthlingborough

CONTENTS

Look what I've found! The author discovers an unrestored privy at Boscobel.

FOREWORD: FROM THE BOTTOM

In an average lifetime, Britons spend more than 186 days just on the loo. Some people have started life on it (Charles V who survived to become Emperor of Germany and Spain) and some die on it (Elvis Presley). All are mightily relieved that it's there!

The week after I was asked to do this book, I was on the QE2 with a group of fellow journalists. Stuck for small talk over dinner one night in the plush Britannia restaurant, I offered 'I've been asked to write a book on Shropshire privies.'

'What's a privy?' asked one sophisticate. 'An outside loo,' I said, 'and I'm not sure where to start.'

An otherwise strong, silent northerner put down his glass and boomed: 'At the bottom, I should think.'

He flushed with success at his own wit. Which was how our journey around the privies of Shropshire – one of the country's largest inland counties – began in the North Sea.

And as soon as I roped in my newspaper and radio pals, to help me dig out local memories and stories, the response was fantastic. I remember driving home from Radio Shropshire after doing a live spot to find a dozen calls already on our answerphone and the radio station swiftly calling with as many again.

Word spread and wherever people were gathered, they also remembered. Despite those who asked 'Is there a call for it?' one thing I very quickly learned is that you can't let all those memories go to waste. They combine to paint a colourful, robust picture of an intimate part of our daily lives. I also came across so many varied tales of days past from real Shropshire characters, that a book on local privies has become very much more than that. Indeed, like outside lavvies themselves, a unique slice of social history.

There was the elderly lady who talked memorably about her 'laying out' days, as everyone from the neighbours to the police used to cry 'Send for Alice' when a dead body needed care and attention. A local vicar got it instantly — he died in her arms.

Another local was enthusiastic about her property-owning great-uncle who would threaten to burn down the closets of his tenants if they didn't pay the rent. I also heard the gory story of one unfortunate who committed suicide behind a privy door and they couldn't get him out.

Although the national habit of popping down the garden is still in living memory, at least a couple of generations know nothing of their grandparents' privy experiences. Brought up with the immaculate ceramics of water closet and bidet, today's children will find it inconceivable that ablutions ever took place in a dark hut, with a man coming along, carrying the residue away and burying it. Or, worse, grandad spread it on the veggie patch. Except that the great organic gardening lobby which is shooting up all around us might well thoroughly approve of that.

Actually, my probings around the darker recesses of our bodily functions unearthed one jolly lady who still uses an earth closet and scoops the remains on to the compost heap. If you didn't know, human waste needs to stay there for two years before use.

Shropshire Privies preserves the memories of Shropshire people as it tells the story of some very special conveniences. Or were they really that convenient at all? Read on.

SHIRLEY TART

[1]

In The Beginning

Well, I never knew that! Something I found myself saying or thinking so many times as I researched this book. It has been a bit like writing two books in tandem – one, a fond and affectionate look back at the Shropshire privies of yesteryear, logging so many memories and checking out current uses for the survivors; the other, a revelation on how human waste has occupied so many for so long, not just individuals dealing with their own, either, but regular brain boxes who made careers out of inventing the best ways to dispose of what everybody produced.

But then, bladder and bowel-emptying is as old as man himself. And while you can accommodate the first without too much of a fandango, the second is a bit different. Though it's odd that with so much ancestral practice, the human race is so very fey and private about bowel habits – admittedly some more than others. Citizens and monks of centuries ago often made a social virtue of going together, you'll read of such examples later. But eventually, Adam and Eve style, we covered ourselves up and by Shakespeare's day, the translation of closet was 'a private room'. So, indeed, it remains.

During these intimate investigations, I got to know the Rev Henry Moule and Thomas Crapper and his predecessors very well indeed. But before any of them came on the scene, others having to deal with the same mess en masse were grappling with the niceties of a sewerage system of sorts. There were times when Britain was in a disgusting and deadly state because of the problems of human waste. If we took a trip through a time warp, we sanitised 21st century folk could not survive our yesterdays.

Waste wasn't that much of a problem when there were only a

7

Ludlow Castle's Garderobe Tower has some splendid examples of long-drop facilities.

Author's delight – long-drop shutes galore!

handful of people to a continent. You just did it and left it. Once it needed dealing with, an early instinct was to bury it. Indeed as a 13-year-old of my acquaintance observed with relish: 'The planet's probably made up of lots of layers of muck.' Probably.

And although today's plumbing for the masses is pretty sophisticated, compared with, say, 200 years ago in Britain, in 2500 BC, the Egyptians were building elaborate bathrooms in the pyramids for their dead to use on the onward journey. And in 1500 BC, on the island of Crete, fresh water sewerage systems and flushing toilets were regularly used.

Travel back to Roman Britain and you'll find very clever systems for public latrines based on the simple logic of drop it down into a brick or stone trench and wash it away in another. Of course where you washed it away to would have also been pretty poisonous. And how awesome are those garderobes where our ancestral lords, their families, servants and many visitors relieved themselves high up inside a castle and the results fell down a shute on the outside, sometimes but not always into a cesspit or moat. Several shutes survive at the 900-year-old Ludlow Castle and both Shropshire-based leading historian Barrie Trinder and his wife Barbara (Ludlow born and a teacher who has taken many a class of wide-eyed pupils on a visit) claim the castle's remains as an excellent example of garderobes.

First referred to in 1138, Ludlow was one of a line of Norman castles along the Marches built to pacify the countryside and hold back the unconquered Welsh. Once a royal property, but owned since the early 1800s by the Earls of Powis, it has its own impressive Garderobe Tower, early 14th century and including several bedrooms, each with its own privy – rare en suites of the day. It's a fascinating thought that they would have been used by Catherine of Aragon who lived at Ludlow's former Norman fortress with her husband Prince Arthur. When Arthur died, Catherine returned to London and married his brother Henry,

Inside Ludlow Castle, did Catherine of Aragon sit on this very spot to do her duty?

soon to stride into history as King Henry VIII. Arthur's heart lies buried in Ludlow, his body at Worcester.

But royal or peasant, rich or poor, everyone had a method – some ingenious, others as basic as you'll get – of dealing with effluent. As we shall see in a minute, there may well have been greater guidance than mere man on this one . . .

For many centuries, the chamber pot, the 'guzunder', was the main indoor receptacle in ordinary households and often merrily emptied through the window, regardless of who was passing by – so the world was definitely ready for a closet genius. Come in, Henry Moule. In his day he was your Mr Earth Closet. And you may well ask what a vicar, son of a solicitor, was doing

11

bothering his head about lavatories. Well, it could be because the reverend gentleman read the Bible a lot.

For instance, Deuteronomy chapter 23 orders us to: 'Designate a place outside the camp where you can go to relieve yourself. As part of your equipment have something to dig with, and when you relieve yourself, dig a hole and cover up your excrement. For the Lord your God moves about in your camp to protect you and to deliver your enemies to you. Your camp must be holy, so that he will not see among you anything indecent and turn away from you.' That's the New International Version, but I prefer the poetry of the King James: 'Thou shalt have a place also without the camp whither thou shalt go forth abroad. And thou shalt have a paddle upon thy weapon. And it shall be, when thou wilt ease thyself abroad, thou shalt dig therewith and turn back and cover that which cometh from thee.'

Rev Moule, born in 1801, was nearly 60 before he finally filled in his cesspool and made his family use buckets, convinced that 'in God's providence there is no waste'. He first buried the sewage in trenches then built a shed, sifted dry earth underneath it and every morning, mixed his prime bucketful with the earth. His later, more sophisticated version of this contraption was a type of commode with a bucket under the seat and a container of the earth (or ashes) behind. When the occupants had gone about their business, they simply pulled a lever and a dollop of the earth dropped into the bucket as discreet camouflage. He discovered that he was producing a good, fertilising manure.

Adam Hart-Davies, who has written books and presented TV programmes about the great eccentrics of lavatories, says that right up to his death in 1880, Rev Moule was still trying to convince the British government that the earth closet was the system of the future. He may well have convinced his Monarch, because Queen Victoria always used one at Windsor Castle even though many types of water closet were by then available.

Walking under open windows used to be a hazardous occupation – as illustrated by Hogarth in 1738.

MOULE'S EARTH CLOSETS

Apparatus on Bearers ready to Fix.
Deal Seat 3' 0" Long.

No. A1724. " Pull Out," as drawn.
No. A1725. " Pull Up " Pattern.
No. A1726. " Self-acting " Pattern.

Strong, Portable, Self-Contained Set. Plain Deal. Galvanized Fittings. Pail complete. 21" Wide. 27" Back to Front.

No. A1727. " Pull Out."
(as drawn)

No. A1728. " Pull Up "

Strong, Portable, Self-contained.
Best Plain Deal.
Fittings of Galvanized Iron.
With Pail complete.

No. A1729. Self-Acting. 21" Wide.
27" Back to Front. 36" High.

No.			
A1724	..	..	57/6
A1725	..	..	70/-
A1726	..	..	100/-
*A1727	..	..	72/6
*A1728	..	..	86/6
*A1729	..	..	102/6

* Pails included.
Other Pails **3/7** Each Extra.

The Rev Henry Moule's earth closets were still popular in the 20th century. This ironmonger's catalogue of 1936 includes the 'self-acting' model (bottom left).

[2]

A ROYAL FLUSH

But water closets for a royal had been around a long time before that. At the end of the 16th century Sir John Harington created what is widely accepted to be the first – for his godmother, Queen Elizabeth I. In fact he had two made, one for himself. He was ridiculed for a daft idea and never repeated it. Nearly 350 years later, in 1848, England chalked up another mark of progress and passed the National Public Health Act. What a moment that was in the history of bums on seats – an expression incidentally with quite a different connotation than the filling of hall, stadium or arena that we use it for today.

The new Act not only became a model plumbing code for the rest of the world, it changed basic lifestyles for millions. It became a legal requirement for every home to have some kind of sanitary facility. It may have been a privy or an ash pit or – glory be – even a flushing toilet. At the same time, the government made available the princely sum of £5 million for sanitary research and engineering, and started building a sewerage system.

However, while we can't imagine in this new, 21st century how we might fare without our sewers, we don't really want to know too much about them, do we? London's underground disposal network may from time to time have been opened to visitors, but the murky world of the sewer is generally beloved only by the rats, the Phantom of the Opera and structural engineers.

And when the revolutionary Act came into being, many people thought the idea was crazy. Moreover, once the facility started to come indoors for everybody, they were even more suspicious. Having lavs in the house like the toffs wasn't healthy.

Curiously enough, one just outside but right by the kitchen door was seen as nastiest of all.

No wonder progress on implementing the new rules was slow. Installing a vast system of sewers was an enormous job as sanitation became the 'It' word. There was still widespread disease and local authorities had their share of headaches. In August 1894, the Wenlock Borough Sanitary District minutes for Madeley record a right old mess. The surveyor reported that he had opened and cleansed an offending culvert at Coalbrookdale but a further burst had taken place 'discharging itself across the highway. The culvert is faulty in construction and connected therewith is four common privies – three belonging to a Mr M. Bailey and one to Mr H. Hughes. It is recommended these should be converted into ventilated traps and pan closets or otherwise disconnected and provided with a watertight cesspit protected from surface and rain water and easy of access for scavenging.'

A year later, the surveyor was asking the authority to serve notices on the owners of the properties at Brown's Row 'to abate the nuisance there by constructing new privies and cesspits at the Gable end of the premises and so as not to abutt upon the public highway.'

It got nastier. The following January, the authority considered an inspector's report of a nuisance at premises belonging to Mr B.Wilcox near Severn Side and occupied by Wm Clay and his wife: 'The living room being crowded out with lumber and filthy accumulations of excreta, decayed food, rags, bones and other offensive matter producing a most fetid atmosphere.'

In Ludlow, the Friar's Cesspool commanded attention from the authorities in 1860 when notice was given to the owners of the property to fill up the cesspool forthwith. And a subsequent minute of the same meeting, recorded in a beautifully bound volume, proved to be a significant moment in Ludlow's history.

THOS. CRAPPER & Co.,

SANITARY ENGINEERS *Ltd.,*

TO

His Majesty the King,

AND

H.R.H. the Prince of Wales.

BY APPOINTMENT.

BY APPOINTMENT.

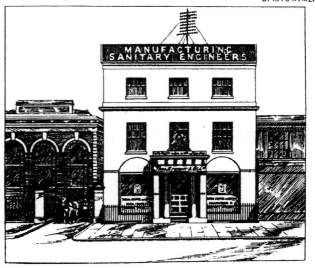

BATHS, LAVATORIES, SINKS, &c.

Show Rooms:

120, KING'S ROAD,

(Opposite Royal Avenue)

CHELSEA, S.W.

Thomas Crapper's flourishing business was awarded four royal warrants.

'It was resolved that the clerk apply to Mr Curlay, Mr Rawlinson and Euston & Amos to know their terms for surveying the town and to report on a system of drainage and water supply to . . .' A fortnight later, it was proposed by the Mayor, seconded by Mr Alderman Marston, 'that it is expedient that the Borough of Ludlow be sewered and drained under the Powers of the Act.' And the following spring, in May 1861, tenders were put out both for the sewers and for a new cattle market for the town.

At about the same time, a young Yorkshireman was making steady progress in the plumbing trade little knowing that he was about to become part of social history – and have his name hijacked in a way he would doubtless never have chosen! Thomas Crapper produced the Silent Valveless Water Waste Preventor which revolutionised the still newfangled, but highly thought of, water closet contraptions of Alexander Cummings and Joseph Bramah by providing effective flushing when the cistern was only half full. Bramah's water closets were so good that the phrase 'what a bramah' entered the language to describe anything of first-rate quality.

As someone with a surname that excites its own comment, I can sympathise with the Crapper family over the manner in which their own name fell into common usage. During World War I, American doughboys spotted 'T.Crapper' on toilet equipment and it wasn't long before they were excusing themselves with the remark 'I'm going to the Crapper.' In no time at all, 'going for a crap' was used as a statement of intent. As well as that, the new word 'crap' was also used to describe a load of rubbish, rotten workmanship, absolutely the pits. Poor Thomas Crapper.

[3]

CLOSET SECRETS

Shropshire certainly had its interesting share of types of outdoor privies – earth, bucket, those with neat, brick-lined drains, Roman-style, and dinky lavvies over water. All had both advantage and disadvantage. The principle of earth privies, where the gubbings dropped into a trench or hole in the ground grandly called a cesspit, might have been environmentally attractive, but cesspits needed to be cleared and that may not have always been quite such fun.

You could measure your challenge when it came to buckets – see exactly what disposal was required. But if buckets overflowed and the nightsoil man (or the next door neighbour for a few bob) was late or you had visitors at a premium moment, buckets were not so good.

The brick-lined drains would carry the residue away by water but if for some reason water became scarce, you were left with a pretty mess. Facilities over moats, streams, open drains or the edge of rivers, however, had a constant water supply to remove the evidence.

Later on, we hear from one lady who remembers vividly what happened when their under-closet stream froze. And in all cases, judged by today's clinical facilities, the final destination of the daily disposal of human waste was lurid.

───────────

Apart from the obvious, what really went on in those little privy buildings and when we'd done what we had to do, how did we clean ourselves? Intriguing questions – and maybe you'll be surprised.

Two and three seaters were places to socialise, catch up on the day or just (as my Grandma Gough used to say about the lavvie) 'to have a minute's peace and quiet'. And in the back-to-back privies of both town and country, conversation was as regular as the clients.

Growing-up daughters would visit to try clandestine cigarettes, read trashy novelettes – often smuggled in up the knicker leg and sometimes left as bum wipers – away from the eyes of strict and chapel-going mothers, practise their singing and prepare enough neatly torn newspaper pieces to last for the next few days.

Many people shared their memories with me of the newspaper used for finishing off the job – an early *Radio Times* was popular – cut into squares, often by the youngsters, a piece of string threaded through and hung on a nail in the whitewashed wall.

Hardly a bidet, this bum fodder, but it served the purpose. And more than one has cuttingly declared during this research, that was about all newspapers were good for.

As a journalist, I've heard all the old jokes about our work ending up as wrappings for fish and chips. How much worse for our professional ancestors – theirs swiftly found its way to the nail on the wall and beyond.

But long before living memory (or newsprint) the vexed question of personal hygiene had occupied the other end of the body – the head. As the population grew, what to do after a visit and what to do with the results was an ongoing problem.

The Romans, efficient and particular folk that they were, used sponges on sticks for cleansing, and scrapers certainly have their place in our privy history. There is also evidence that in medieval England straw was used, but it may have been more for dropping onto the privy's contents than dealing with bums.

Fred Thomas's three-seater at Alberbury was handy – he had three daughters.

Pieces of cloth from monks' habits were the loo paper of their time in priories. The genesis of the expression 'dirty habits'?

A number of dig-outs have found enough moss in cesspits to indicate a soft option and ladies with access to silky bird feathers would favour a handful of those. Ticklish one, that. Grass was undoubtedly an early favourite and so was anything like dock or vegetables with similar shaped leaves. Only recently, a vigorous walker of my acquaintance told me how he'd been caught short on a brisk hike across Shropshire's Long Mynd and had to resort to a handful of leaves – which out of consideration to the sheep eyeing him balefully, he'd then buried. He was quite proud of himself when I pointed out that he was merely following in the noble footsteps of his ancestors.

In more recent years, quite often a trip down the garden would see people carrying their own favourite wherewithal to complete the operation. Precious tissue paper, saved from presents, was highly prized, some sweetie papers definitely had what it took and there was certainly a preference when it came to newspapers.

For example, not the *Daily Telegraph*, one who remembers tells me – not because of its texture but because the ink came off on your bum. He was also at pains to point out that his wife took the paper home from her cleaning job, he didn't want anybody to think he'd bought it or, worse, read it!

Toilet paper was available for the better off, by then. It was developed by the British Perforated Paper Company in 1880 but would hardly have been the soft and pastel coloured variety beloved by those TV puppies today. And the lowly still had to put up with other ingenious wipes for years after that.

[4]

GRACIOUS LIVING

It was common for castles and big manor houses to have several privies round and about the grounds which they used in 'progression'. When one was full, if they didn't have another home to live in, the whole family simply moved on to the next lavvie in rotation – until somebody came to empty them. At moated homes and farms, long-drop equipment would send privy contents straight down into the moat. A modern-day visit to such a property provides gruesome excitement for the imagination.

And so to Moat Farm. It stands where it's stood for centuries between the tiny villages of Stapleton and Pulverbatch and it was there that current guardian, Pearl Mottram, led me to Shropshire's only surviving complete moat.

There has been a dwelling on this site since 1089. The ancient brick-built privy emptied its offerings into the moat until the Mottram family got indoor facilities in the 1960s – it was long since dried out by then, of course. The two-seater privy also has a patch of wattle and daub set in otherwise red plaster. And the contents of the privy slipped merrily away down the brick-built 'shute'. Pearl chuckles: 'I remember our son Michael coming home from boarding school for the weekend and bringing a friend with him. The lad was amazed, he couldn't believe you had to go so far from the house and on one occasion he slipped and fell down. He came back covered in mud. Good job they were only home for the weekend.' What about clearing out the residue in those later years when the water had long since gone?

Pearl said briskly: 'Oh it was just left there to rot away.'

Cracking apple tree country!

Grin and bear it. Pearl Mottram at Moat Farm, Pulverbatch has some happy memories of her privy – they used it until the 1960s.

24

Lid up at Moat Farm revealing the efficient brick-lined shute to take it all away.

The massive Moat Farm wall clearly shows the depth of the moat and the open ground its width.

A couple of villages away at Moat Hall, farmers Martin and Helen Davies are immensely proud of their two-hole, two-tier family privy. The house is around 1600, the privy could be about the same.

When I think of some of the little gems and old relics into which I squeezed, trusty camera at the ready, this one was big enough for an afternoon stroll!

The heavy oak seat is very old, if not original, handsome with elaborate moulding and will have nursed bottoms galore over the centuries. Maybe including the clerical bum of one Bishop Berington who used to live at the hall. More recently, it was certainly a facility for men from a local one-time colliery. A couple of them went visiting recently and reported that they'd spent many a happy hour there.

26

Helen and Martin Davies are very proud of their Moat Hall privy.

Martin and his father before him have done a lot of work on the building, including replacing the floor with the sort of massive oak railway sleepers which will see out all of us. While a little domestic graffiti of its day on the wall behind the seat proclaims 'Me and my wife' – and they've carefully framed it with glass for posterity.

The lavatory's long-drop system was right up against the moat – filled in eventually with council rubbish – which they'd actually like to restore and Martin is pretty certain that, as you'd expect, the water ran underneath and carried off the deposits. There's also a room below which Martin remembers crawling into as a lad and fetching out eggs from the straw which by then was piled there. Now, Helen has cleared it all out and with a pair of curtains at the entrance, it makes a 21st century playhouse for their young daughter!

The Lander family was knitted into the fabric of last century Wellington. And when Joan Lander died and willed Sunnycroft to the National Trust, she handed over a unique slice of Edwardian history.

Apart from the furniture, furnishings, conservatory, greenhouses all pretty well date-stamped, the outside lavatory is tucked away in a courtyard behind the back door, a bit off the Sunday afternoon tourist beat. In fact the National Trust people on the gate didn't know anything about it.

Fortunately I found Joel. He's the gardener and he escorted me through a back yard gate, beyond the modern loos and to the one in question. It was the first I'd found with a ceramic pan instead of a dented bucket or an earth job. Joel said it had been used by gardeners until just a couple of years ago. He also pointed out that there was a great space above it, like an open loft, and nobody knew why. Even the Mars bar wrapper in the pan wasn't really a clue!

Another 'grand' house with a loo and a view was a former gentleman's residence, now a working farm, set high above Oswestry in borderland country. Built in massive pieces of grey stone, probably local, it's an 18th century monument with quite a history. From the house, you walk – very carefully – down ancient steps, past the greenhouse and over ruts and mounds, alongside part of a wall in the same stone. Round the corner at the end of it, eureka! We see an ancient, crudely fashioned three-seater, just a trio of holes in a plank, and peering into the dark and gloomy (though decent sized) privy, what looks like a set of coat hooks hanging on the wall behind. What sophistication! On the other side of that wall, a modern-day lavatory in the farmyard caters for the outdoor workers. But the centuries-old facility helps paint this social picture of how our ancestors lived in undoubtedly harder days.

Sunnycroft's Victorian one-seater was used by gardeners until recently. The vast space above it is a mystery.

[5]

A MEDLEY OF MEMORIES

We live in an old Abraham Darby house – built as a nailmaker's cottage – in the heart of the area of industrial change, where the world's first iron bridge was spawned and now a World Heritage site.

In our garden we have our own slice of privy history. The driveway and top lawn is on one level, the house on the next and the shed lower still. Alongside one quaint set of wooden railway sleeper steps is a brick-built, tiled building which mimics the original 1812 part of the house. It has the same quarry tiling as our kitchen and garden room floors. And the name 'Inky' is scrawled on the brick above the old door. Now another log shed, it has certainly been a dog kennel – Inky perhaps – and a previous owner, who lived in the house for 25 years, confirms that it was once the closet.

Just a few miles away between the old pit township of Dawley (on which Telford New Town was based) and market town of Wellington, Lawley village has seen enormous change with new fast roads, motorways and acres of housing around it. But its core remains intact. John Churm lives at Glendale opposite a former farmhouse, built between 1730 and 1750 and developed into four cottages when Abraham Darby himself took on the project. John's grandparents lived at what is now Yew Tree Cottage; they probably moved in 1932 and John has known the former farm all his life. Happily for us, in 1969, when the old brick-built privy with its tiled roof was still there, John decided to take some pictures of the relic.

'It used to have the little wooden seat, but that was nearly

The author's own privy building which has possibly since housed a pig, certainly a dog – Inky – and which now protects logs for the fire.

31

John Churm of Lawley took this privy snap of his granny's convenience, now gone, when he was a lad.

gone even then and there were plum trees and lots of other garden plants and trees outside. It was lovely really. Now you're going to ask me how far it was from the house, aren't you?'

I was.

'Well here's another picture. I think I took this one from by the plum tree looking back towards the house.'

A long way from the house!

As so often was the case, it was pretty nearly a bicycle ride away!

Talking of which, a young Dawley woman, visiting her friend a couple of generations ago, suddenly saw a head bobbing up and down outside the kitchen window. Alarmed, she asked who on earth it was. Everybody else was unfazed. It was just the son of

33

the house going about his daily business – and tackling the long haul of the allotment-style plot between the back door and the privy, on his bike.

Who said romance is dead? So asks Janet Eatough, now living in the market town of Wellington. Her experience with outside facilities was a real learning curve – and she is the only proud owner I found who got a privy as a present . . . ribbon wrapped!

Janet says: 'When I got married in 1955, I went to live in a cottage at the bottom of the drive to Whitley Manor at Pulstone near Newport. My husband was the farm manager for Mr E.Watson-Jones. There was no water in the cottage, we had a deep well in the back yard.

'Water was heated by lighting a stone-built boiler in the kitchen (lovely in winter, agony in summer) and baths taken in a tin bath (Wellington market, five shillings or 25p) by the front room fire. Hair was washed in rainwater from a butt, complete with insect larvae and bits and pieces of anything that had fallen in.

'The biggest shock was the earth closet at the bottom of the garden. It was a brick-built hut with a two-hole wooden seat scrubbed smooth and polished by generations of bottoms. Next door's was joined on to ours by a wooden partition.

'The main problem for me, was fear – fear of the long journey in the dark, the oak tree nearby with an owl in it, scufflings in the hedge, whether someone was lurking in the loo or if the one next door was being used and I might be heard. So many fears. But a great cure for constipation. One hoot from the owl . . . and all was well.

'BUT . . . on my 21st birthday, my husband of eight months gave me the best of all presents. An Elsan toilet.

'He had cleaned out the coal house, lime washed it, built a concrete plinth and installed the chemical toilet. There was even a ribbon round it and I used it first!'

Joan Bright, who now lives over the border in Powys, tells of a privy reunion she wasn't expecting.

Her mother was born in 1894 and was nearly 100 when she died. She lived with her family – name of Ewels – on a big estate at Atcham near the county town of Shrewsbury, where her father was gamekeeper and bailiff. Joan, formerly a Shropshire Evans, says: 'At 18 mother was asked to go to help an aunty who was unwell. This aunt and uncle farmed at Clun or just outside. My mother had to cook for the men, do the washing and the hundred and one jobs there are to do on a farm.

'It was here that she first saw the privy over the stream. She told me there were two holes in the seat and you could sit on one and fish in the other. I don't think hygiene was uppermost in their minds.

'As a child, I was intrigued by this story, visualising a bridge like the one in the willow pattern, over a stream, with a sort of Portaloo perched on it.

'Many years later, I married a farmer and one day we had occasion to go to that farm at Clun to buy a clock. I told the owner about my mother's story. And would you believe, he took me out into the garden to what looked like a shed.

'On opening the door, there was the very privy (with water gurgling under it) which she had described all those years before.'

Jancis Mander has lived in Shropshire since being evacuated there from Coventry on the day war broke out. Her father, the Rev Charles Dodd, was vicar of Eaton Constantine and Leighton, her mother headmistress of Leighton school. Jancis and her husband, now Shropshire Crown Court judge Michael Mander, have lived for most of their married life in the next village of Garmston. But her memories of rough and ready facilities remain vivid.

Brave beyond belief. Jancis Mander valiantly fought her way through the ivy, rediscovering the Leighton privies of her youth.

The remains of a pair of old privies – ivy covered and pretty – can still be seen alongside the road through Leighton, opposite the Kynnersley Arms pub. I was told they were once sheds. Still curious, I asked my friend Jancis about them. 'Definitely the privies to the old village hall,' she said briskly. 'I can tell you that for certain – I've used them.'

The old facilities are now on the land of White House Farm but Jancis remembers: 'If we had a dance in the hall, that's where we had to go. There was a gents across the road at the pub but not a ladies. The outside block was in use until 1960 when the new hall was built.'

But for her and many more, an evening tripping the light fantastic didn't compensate for the scary trips which became necessary after too many glasses of lemonade. And 'visits' at home weren't much better, either. Jancis recalls: 'At the School House, Leighton, where I lived for six years, I dreaded having to visit the privy – our only lavatory – because I hate spiders and the dark! There was no electric light so we had to take a torch at night after plucking up courage to go out at all. If the torch failed there was a panic at the thought of all the big spiders crawling around, and it was always cold.

'The bucket was emptied every week by the school caretaker's husband into a deep pit in our garden. Every so often, the big boys from the school were put to dig a new one. And once while watching them, my sister fell in the full one up to her neck. She was pulled out by the strongest boy. The caretaker's husband also emptied the two buckets at the school – into the brook about 100 yards away.

'I was lucky to live next to the school so didn't have to go to those "offices" as we called the lavatories. And the girls who did were not pleased when they found the boys looking up from below where the buckets were in a kind of cellar. There was the ruler for those boys who were found out – but they still did it!'

The Squatter's Cottage at Blists Hill, which once housed numerous little children, also has a matching privy and pigsty. A quiet moment in the lavvie (left) with a couple of contented Saddlebacks or Whites snuffling next door, what more could you ask?

Could this be the same naughty schoolboy activity on which Norman Angell looks back with such affection? Different village, similar time but, by chance, he and Jancis eventually ended up at grammar school together.

Norman says: 'At our small school in Kemberton, the privies were not over-refined. Hinged doors at the back of the girls' lav permitted the removal of buckets. It was known for some over inquisitive boys to mis-use these doors. But woe betide any offender caught by the ever vigilant headmistress, Miss Wallace.'

As the many fans of Ken Dodd will know, he is very fond of recalling that, in his day, everybody had to be good singers so that their necessary visits were not disturbed by others in a

Easy does it ... what's in there? Norman Angell investigates his cousin David's old privy in Donington.

hurry, thinking the privy was empty. Ken now has a home near Whitchurch in Shropshire – with proper plumbing! Norman remembers that his family had to be good singers for the same reason as there was no lock on their privy door. He recalls: 'The lav was at the end of the garden, a good 25 yards from the house. The suite of buildings comprised the aforesaid lav, and what had been a pigsty. What a haven for flies this was in its glory days. Perhaps that was why the ensemble was screened by old rambler roses, gorgeously scented pale pink beauties whose perfume must have had to work overtime.

'Ours was a wide, two-seater affair often visited after the fall of darkness when a rickety candle-burning lantern would light our way. And when it got too hot, burn our fingers. The occasional shovelful of agricultural lime was the Harpic of its day.'

Norman also took me out to his cousin's house at Sydnal Lane, in Donington, near Albrighton. Pat and David Cooke inherited the facilities when they constructed their splendid house from old cottages. Now one of the grand old wrecks has snapdragons over the roof, holly at the entrance and another is a blaze of cotoneaster flowers in season with sweet smelling lilacs close by for a particular purpose. Floral ways and happy days!

Privies could be handy little hiding places sometimes, as well. Joy Minton from Shifnal recalls the time she and her brother found a shilling. The siblings from the Bebb family farm in Wellington spent the lot on sweets. As Joy says, a bob was a big chunk of a weekly wage packet in those days and they knew they couldn't explain away that amount of confectionery so they hid them in the closet.

But on a necessary visit himself, Father Bebb found the sweets, was horrified at what they'd spent and the youngsters were in real trouble.

[6]

THE MUCK MEN

Clearing out has been a major matter down the ages. The unpleasant job of cleaning medieval cesspits was carried out by valiant fellows called rakers or gongfermors – and we read of one poor man, Richard the Raker, who in 1326 fell through the rotten timbers of his privy, drowning 'monstrously in his own excrement'. In more recent times, there was a network of arrangements to keep the tidal wave of human waste on the move.

With the farthest flung country privies, it wasn't such a big deal. If nobody else emptied your buckets or cesspits, you just dumped the contents on the allotment. But in more urban areas, the nightsoil man was your fellow. The job was a well enough known one in Shropshire, yet the people who did it remain more or less a mystery – hardly anybody admits to seeing them – some locals I questioned were alarmingly prudish about bodily functions at all and few admit to having known nightsoil men, let alone be related to them.

But they must have had relatives. Even Jackie Hadley, the Muck Man, who was actually a daytime phenomenon. He had quite a reputation in the small pit and steel town of Dawley and its surrounding villages. Jackie kept his cart and his horse, Dolly, at the bottom of the fir trees on Dawley's Paddock Mount. One popular memory says he lived in an old cottage by the Wide Waters, another that his cottage was next to Durnall's shop on Portley Corner, opposite Dolly's stabling.

I'm part of the second crew and can just remember him as small, hunched up, bowed from bucket carrying, perhaps. Others say he was frighteningly large. So many people contacted

41

me about Jackie, I thought I was going to find a wealth of tales. But almost all of them simply recalled how scared they were of him. Whether that was to do with the job he did, or the manner in which he did it, isn't clear. The local rhyme (called after him at a safe distance) was 'Jackie Hadley sells fish, three halfpence a dish, don't buy it, don't buy it, it stinks when you fry it.' As far as anybody knows he never did sell fish. He'd have made an unlikely costermonger.

A couple of local lads (now elderly men) recall how they would wait until Jackie had hobbled away, leaving Dolly and cart behind a long row of terraced houses. Just as he was coming back, laden down with two full buckets, the rascals would whisper to the horse, 'come on Dolly, come on.' And the amiable mare would trundle off, cart behind her, to the other end of the village, leaving a furious Jackie stranded with his unsavoury load.

Both sets of my grandparents lived in the crooked, L-shaped scar of cottages called Dark Lane, several winding, rural miles from Dawley. Every house had a privy at the bottom of the garden and the whole village became a much mourned victim of Telford New Town's early infrastructure. I was born over the bridge, past Payne's shop, up the hill at number 17, Malinslee – once the modern centre of a late 20th century new town was established, I learned with dismay that I was really born on Carrefour car park. Surely not in a trolley!

But long before the new town, we moved to live in Dawley, leaving our rural cottage with side by side lavvies in the garden opposite the blackberry bushes (one for us, one for the neighbours) and we inherited indoor plumbing. Indeed TWO brand new ceramic loos – one in the bathroom, one downstairs. Posh indeed.

Which is where we kids came across Jackie Hadley. We didn't need him professionally by then, of course. But, according to my

Jackie Hadley's partner Jack Ferriday (right) and the cleansing gang, including Jack's son Billy (front). His grandson Mike Shepherd doesn't know who the other three are, but Jackie Hadley isn't among them. Shame!

mother, Jackie visited one day to say that our old dog had chased and bitten him. He couldn't have been all bad because when presented with the old girl for inspection, he said that no, it wasn't her. Sighs of relief and a pungent memory of Jackie's sackcloth apron or overall, definitely on a high when it came to odour. As a nipper, I remember standing behind him in Mrs Durnall's (food) shop on one of his working days.

Phew! Strong stuff.

Mike Shepherd's grandad Jack Ferriday was one of Jackie's partners in this murky work. 'He had the horse and I think the cart was called a drugger. It was the shape of a bowl with a lid in the middle. They used to have buckets of you know what, thick 'uns and thin 'uns, to put on the garden,' Mike says colourfully. Not only does he remember it, he has a picture of Grandad Ferriday and his cleansing gang, including his son (Mike's Uncle Billy). We thought for a moment we'd found Jackie but no such luck. He, poor chap, remains a distant figure, but always terrifying in the memory of those he served.

Rita Mulcahy (Rich as was) spotted my privy activities on a Shropshire website from her home in South Australia. Married to an Aussie, she has lived Down-Under for many years. But Salopians will remember her dad, Alderman Joe Rich, who served two terms as mayor of the old Borough of Wenlock in the 1950s. Apart from her memories of the mysterious nightsoil man, who visited early for emptying duties when the family lived at Strethill Road, Dale End, Rita also remembers her father coming to the rescue in a big way.

'We had an earth privy with quite a large hole – terrifying for a child. I sat in there one day and accidentally dropped in my little kitten. I had taken him in for company and he squirmed out of my grasp. But my father, always resourceful, lifted him out on the long-handled dustpan and washed him off very efficiently.'

One hero alderman and one messy but very much alive puss!

Half a world away, she also put me in touch with her friend Trevor Bagley who, it turned out, lives less than a mile down the valley from us! Trevor confesses that he's old enough to remember the outside privies – though he was one of the lucky lads in the Dale, they had a modern, flush one.

'But we also had a redundant, outside job, just a few yards away from the house. We used to keep chickens in it. I think that it was a one-seater and I remember a large lilac bush or tree nearby and planted there for obvious reasons. I think that this must have been a fashionable, upmarket extra,' he chuckled.

44

[7]

M USEUM   P IECES

You don't need much imagination as the west wind whistles across the Wroxeter plain in sight of the Wrekin and east of the county town of Shrewsbury. You can pretty well feel the draught that those second century Viroconium citizens would have known as they lined up to relieve themselves at the bath house latrine. Draughts were not all, either. This particular and mundane bodily function was as matey an affair as everything else which took place in the magnificent public baths. From the huge, aisled exercise hall, through the well-named frigidarium, tepidarium, steam rooms, and the piscina (open air pool), the emphasis was on three things – fitness, cleanliness and the pursuance of your social life. So in this fourth largest city in Roman Britain, bathers obeying the call of nature carried on gossiping, doing deals or even discussing civic matters. Nearly 2,000 years later, the latrine block at Wroxeter Roman City is on the tourist run with visitors from all over the world peering curiously into its deep, stone-lined drains, imagining our ancestors literally going about their business.

And as they've steadily unearthed the remains of Viroconium, we marvel again at the sophisticated plumbing of Roman Britain. In this case, an aqueduct brought the water supply from the Bell Brook. It was just a simple but effective open channel which was clay-lined and followed the natural contours of the terrain to provide a head of water and a reception tank (castellum aquae). The supply was continuous with more than was needed for the baths, domestic users, storage tanks or fountains.

The water had to overflow somewhere, which was good news

The author can't believe it. Did my Roman ancestors really sit here?

for hygiene – it was used to flush the main sewers under the seats and so carried the waste clear of the city. The latrines lie almost alongside the remnants of the old Roman road (Watling Street) from London to Holyhead with some of the sewers found during excavation turning out to be bigger and more impressively complex than imagined. At certain times of day, householders were also allowed to flush their private sewers and, here, those under one group of houses could be flushed from a water main which ran along the side of the street. Yes, sewer-ownership was pretty big business in Roman Britain!

Hundreds of years later, in 1649, Prince Charles, eventually King Charles II, was routed in battle at Worcester and fled north-west towards Shropshire. He stopped off variously at Boscobel House, White Ladies Priory, half a mile away, and travelled in secret (and on foot) to Madeley about nine miles from Boscobel, all to stake his claim to the throne and to avoid the fate of his father Charles I – he'd been beheaded. At Boscobel he hid in an attic and then he went outside and climbed an oak tree to avoid being caught by Cromwell's soldiers. He and a faithful companion spent at least one day there (Saturday, September 6th) in some considerable discomfort but relative safety. The tree became known as The Royal Oak and remains a major attraction for today's 22,000 visitors a year to Boscobel.

Encouraged by this great inheritance of secrecy, hiding places and intrigue, Boscobel retains its share of rumour and speculation. Did that small door at the base of a chimney stack in the first floor Squire's Room conceal a secret cavity? Hardly, it's the first place any serious searcher would have looked.

It's much more likely that the space in the stack was originally used as an earth closet or privy. With the small door simply the access point for cleaning out the bottom of the stack. Mundane or what?

47

As Mary says at Boscobel: 'Guess what they did here.'

Outside there are three brick-built privies (each a two-seater). In recent years, an architect working on the building suggested that they should be tidied up because they'd make a nice 'extra' for visitors to see. So two sets got the full treatment for the tourist trail with the inevitable question as to whether the royal bum of Charles II had ever sat on one of the holes in the wooden planks. Again, hardly. These were a good couple of hundred years after him; the little brick-built closets are typically 19th century.

But if he never got the chance to avail himself of that facility, modern-day visitors did.

Glory be! No sooner were Boscobel's last century privies

48

unveiled as typical of their time, than people started using them. English Heritage guide Mary Gough says indignantly: 'At that point we thought "Oh no, you don't" and we stopped leaving them open. But you should see what somebody did in a Priest's Hole in the house.'

At which point I make my excuses and go back outside!

Mary says: 'The Evans family, who were big manufacturers from Derbyshire, lived here then. This was their summer holiday home and they had a very big family so would have probably used all the privies.'

The first two-seater is just off the farmyard which has a 17th century barn but is otherwise mostly 19th century including a farmhouse of the period. Once inside the brick-built loo, neat little lids fit over the two holes, and a good look through the gloom reveals not only a happy colony of whopping spiders, but a shaft of light down below which leads to a cesspit behind the privy. Walk round to the back and see quite clearly how simple but efficient was the system to empty the residue and haul it across to the dung heap.

The privy in the corner of the formal garden is built onto the corner of the main house, with a discreet, walled approach. Almost the all-mod-cons of its day.

The last of Boscobel's little trio of outdoor conveniences is beyond the tearooms, up an old-fashioned garden path, and since it never was restored it has an ancient, paintless wooden door and several tons of wonderful leaf mould on the floor which has fermented for years and which I nearly bagged up for the roses.

It was all as any old-fashioned, down-the-garden cottage privy, left to its own devices, might have ended up. I loved it. For the record, the real 21st century loos for visitors are in the restored stable block!

The authentic doctor's surgery at Blists Hill boasts a privy in the back yard – a very spick, span and repaired one, with foliage and sweet-smelling shrubs in attendance.

One Shropshire township has two outdoor privies on opposite sides of the dust track road, both attached to pigsties each of which house a couple of rare breed pigs. One lot pink, the other black! Both privies still have the single seat plank fitted inside. And there is yet another neat little brick-built hut, tidied up in the modern way, in the yard of the doctor's consulting room.

What a find for the privy searcher. But this is a very different town from today's modern sprawls or high rise blocks. Here, most people are dressed in Victorian clothes, run Victorian shops and businesses and spend their days in 19th century houses. At Blists Hill open air museum, the past unrolls and visitors are welcome day by day to recall the living conditions of their ancestors. The sprawling, last-century town contains many buildings from industrial east Shropshire and beyond. Like an 1830 Squatter's Cottage from Burrough's Bank at nearby Little Dawley (my home village for 20 years). The tiny cottage was moved to Blists Hill complete with old stone-built privy and pigsty.

The Victorian lookalike at the cottage was fascinated that I was intrigued with old lavatories and announced: 'My 90-year-old aunt still has one. She used to keep a turkey in it.'

A distinctively shaped Toll House, taken brick by brick from the A5 just outside Shrewsbury and rebuilt at the musuem, also has its brick lavvie and pigsty. And while it might never have been fresh as a daisy, it does boast a vertical natural air vent above the seat. I heard a few tales about these – and about cheeky lads peering through. Like the Squatter's Cottage, the Toll House privy is whitewashed inside with just enough room for one person at a time to be private.

Blists Hill also has a splendid old pharmacy where you could have queued for your ground medication or sat in the scary chair to have a tooth out with terrifying looking instruments. The pharmacy houses a wonderful selection of chamber pots and

51

The Toll House at Blists Hill: if not a place to linger, the air vent above the seat helped.

Those were the days! Cure-all for anything from throats and colds to head and stomach ailments, but in the absence of modern-day facilities the portable pots were always handy.

pans of days gone by as a reminder of how the deeds were done in granny's day.

The first religious community at Haughmond Abbey probably settled there towards the end of the 11th century. By 1135, it was established as a house of Augustinian canons. What is left of the great medieval abbey, house and church tells the story of centuries of praise, worship and simple monastic life in one remote Shropshire spot, now just over three miles north of Shrewsbury.

The 14th century abbot's hall and the skeleton of the magnificent west window are awesome – so are some of the more mundane aspects of Haughmond Abbey.

There was an 18-seater reredorter (communal latrine) now identified only by the sturdy, stone-lined drain and the walls of the basement which have well stood the test of time.

The floor would have been higher then and the seats built up at the top of the drain. All used and manned by our medieval ancestors.

Some, so far as English Heritage's Val Jones is concerned, with us still.

No nonsense, down-to-earth Val has helped look after Haughmond for several seasons and swears she's seen the lowly monk whose job it was to empty the latrines. 'He was walking along, all hunched up, looking down and pushing a wheelbarrow,' she said. And as a graphic afterthought: 'Fancy spending eternity pushing poo.'

Val first saw the wheelbarrow-pushing monk fleetingly but quite clearly, then for longer when she whipped through the timewarp again. In a place so steeped in history, could this have been a trick of the imagination? Certainly not, says Val.

Those many centuries ago, her modest, brown-clad monk seemed to be charged with taking latrine deposits to the large

Val Jones and the amazing 18-holer at Haughmond Abbey. She claims to often see the monk who emptied the reredorter.

cloister and digging them in as a robust fertiliser for the vegetables. But there is more. The canons, priests and abbots buried their important dead in the large cloister as well, to also be gently nurtured by the contents of the facilities over which they may so lately have sat, even produced. A clear case of getting your own back.

Finally . . . St Andrew's church in Shifnal is more than 900 years old and has a priest's loo halfway up the spiral staircase to the Parvis Room. Many modern-day worshippers think it's always been a sort of store cupboard! But visiting clergy would actually live in the Parvis Room and the poky facility with its small drainage hole brought sighs of clerical relief. All these years on, the church recently built a new loo, meeting room and kitchen. While most worshippers are also mightily 'relieved' at this, a few still think self-discipline should be exercised because bladders and bowels are not for emptying in the precincts of the church!

[8]

PRIVIES TODAY

Would our ancestors ever have believed the good housekeeping stories of what today's owners do with the privy at the bottom of the garden?

In 21st century Shropshire, those which have stood the test and not been chopped up for firewood are variously used for logs, coal, garden tools and as a sleepover for the dogs. Some have housed a pig, I heard of one which is often home to a peacock and one, previously mentioned, which housed a turkey. It's not unusual for rabbits to use an old loo as a hutch – though I couldn't find any who still did – and stories of rats in the (albeit unused) drainage systems were pretty frequent as well.

I soon learnt to approach a privy building, open the door (if there) and peer down the hole with great caution. Especially when my escorts were a worrying distance behind me!

Less worryingly, children's playhouses are a favourite new use and – yes, all right – some of yesterday's lavatories are absolute rubbish dumps.

One grateful owner thanked me profusely for motivating her to clear it out. That's my pleasure. Because until they did have a sort-out on my behalf, several people didn't even know that the privy 'fittings' were still in there, nailed down plank seats being removed to reveal near-perfect, if neglected underpinnings.

Roger and Sue Norry have lived in Spring Village at Horsehay since the 1980s. Along with their (probably 19th century) home, they inherited the brick-built privy complete with its own original concrete path to make the going easy. Today, it's sited in an attractive courtyard behind their house. Roger had thought he'd probably strip out the inside and use the old lavatory for storage. Then he realised it was a bit daft to dump a little slice of social history. Why not restore it? So that's what he did.

Thanks, Roger. You've made a great contribution to *Shropshire Privies*.

Someone had indeed nailed down the lid of the adult two-seater, so when Roger carefully undid it, all was preserved. At the foot of the left hand hole is a baby seat in the same original pine. Roger says: 'I just cleaned it, rubbed it down and repaired part of it round the frame.'

The result is museum stuff. The privy walls are whitewashed as in days of yore, there's an authentic candle on the sill of the tiny window and the original door is being restored.

The sewerage system seemed to be an old stone drain running beneath metal panels to one side of the privy which Roger found and removed. What a thrill to find among all the great has-beens, a real privy restored!

Indeed more owners of the former mundane facilities are catching the privy restoration bug, and looking out for grants or schemes to help.

Early one Saturday morning, Linda Clutterbuck of Glebe Farm at Cound walked me across a small rotovated field to a fine example standing in splendid isolation a sharp sprint from the house – a strong candidate for the loo with the view title.

The house (they no longer farm there) is 1701, Grade 2 listed. And while there is no information to hand on the age of the tiled-roof privy, it's undoubtedly old. Above the two-seat plank is a round, porthole-style window where Linda's husband fitted a perspex circle – for the goats to look through. Yes, they were closet inhabitants, too. 'We don't have them any more but they sort of lived in here and loved looking through the window,' Linda says affectionately.

It's a picture! No effort was spared by Roger and Sue Norry at Horsehay –
and the result is an added attraction to the family garden.

One for him, one for her and one for baby.

Interestingly, the outside pump once used for a well is also listed and Linda wonders when it came to gradings, why the pump and not the privy? Given the resources, she would love to tackle a restoration job.

A few miles away in Park Lane, Madeley, Alison Wood and Richard Norbury have been in their 1836 home for nearly three years.

Their little corner privy tucked away in a pretty garden was overgrown when they found it. They have opened it up, built a step down and, tongue-in-cheek, added a neat little 'out of order' sign. The seating plan is an unusual, keyhole-shaped one-holer. Richard and Alison would also like to do more to restore or preserve but as ever for those of us with old houses, there is always something which seems to have a greater priority – like your roof, your drains, your electrics.

When it comes to the old-time facilities, Richard says: 'I had already wondered whether there were any grants available for them because rebuilding in brick and tile can be very expensive. It seems a shame that even those left might be neglected because people can't afford to restore them.'

As someone who has just stumbled across a wonderful slice of our domestic history, I'd totally agree with that.

Mike and Kate Taylor at Dovehill Cottage in Willey have their loo propped up in a novel way – by a massive tree growing through it. A mechanical frog croaks merrily at the garden gate, the view is woodland and (croaking frog apart) all is at peace.

Part of the former woodcutter's cottage on Lord Forester's estate is 16th century, the rest was built when there was a tax on bricks. Bigger bricks meant less tax. The outside privy and wash house were built at least 200 years ago. The wooden com-

A distinctive keyhole seat at Park Lane, Madeley may have been arty but what did it do to your bum?

plex confirms that somebody used vast half rounds of wood long before we thought we'd invented them, and it is held up by a long established hydrangea. Kate says she doesn't know what would happen if the tree fell down. It would be the end of an era, I guess. The one-seater bench is still there in the privy's gloom, with the space in front now used for coal. The adjoining wash house has a copper and boiler and an ancient sink with a water tap. Outside – with their many grandchildren in mind – Mike has fixed a false door on the side of the lavatory to make the building look like a little woodland house. He's added

Wow! A massive tree holds up Mike and Kate Taylor's privy at Willey.

Still room to sit comfortably!

gnomes, a fairy garden ... and the old Willey privy lives again for 21st century children.

We stake claim to medieval Much Wenlock as our nearest market town. Though, in truth, we don't visit often enough. But it's always a pleasure to take a little step back in time, whatever the reason. Today, the reason is lavatories.

Behind her lovely 1415 town-centre home, June Cox has a pair of semis tucked into the corner of a private garden. The house was once a pair of cottages, so one privy apiece.

Work has been done to tidy up the little bit of history and make the old building safe, helped by an ingenious metal contraption. June would like to see them restored.

One still has an ancient door with an opening at the top but looking as though it's been chewed at the bottom. We won't ponder by whom. Or what.

I had great fun finding what can only be described as a 'lavatory block' out at West House, Chirbury. The stone part of the house is about 300 years old, the rest is Victorian, about 1850s, and Dorothy Fleming enthusiastically guided me round the outdoor facilities. There's a three-seater on the corner of the block which we photographed by clever use of Dorothy's long torch, and a single-seater round the corner alongside another wooden door which revealed the cleaning part of the operation, the pit, with its metal emptying mechanism – pretty sophisticated for its day, I'd say. Lathe and plaster ceilings, ornate pieces of wood and robustly solid seats all add their own interest.

It's always a treat to sit down with farmer Frank Dakin and hear his Shropshire tales of yesteryear. So we cleared the grand-children's toys from the outside privy and talked about that!

Frank and his wife Anne live at Drayton Lodge just outside

Shifnal in a fine 1760 house. They moved from Brewer's Oak Farm a mile up the road, now farmed by their son, Young Frank and his family. There is nothing which Frank Snr doesn't know about the houses, the land or the surrounding area.

The privy, he says, would be about 1870; their wonderful cheese room which now makes a great spot for big-time entertaining, was built around the same time. 'The privy would have been needed for all the people who worked on the farm then – a lot more than these days. Irish people used to come and work here for instance, potato picking,' says Frank. Now, the old loo lives again as a place of fun to share with the grandchildren.

Over in Alberbury on the Welsh side of Shrewsbury, there was no nightman needed for farmer Fred Thomas. He used to empty his trio of wooden seater privies himself – by shovelling them out and spreading the residue across his fields. Muck spreading in the true sense. For my visit all these years later, proud Fred had cleared out the lavatories – literally down the garden at Lower Wood Farm – painted the seat and door frame a rich, rust red and given the inside a coat of white distemper as well.

But that wasn't always his task: 'When I was a kid, it was the maid's job to regularly come and paint the toilet,' said Fred.

His three daughters found the loo convenient in every way – they could all visit together! One of them, Jean, is now the tenant at the farm and Fred lives next door.

As a final flourish in social history statistics, Fred's son-in-law, Shrewsbury solicitor Chris Wilson, reckons it was quite common to find someone dead in the outside privy early on a winter morning. No doubt to do with feeling ill and having to stagger downstairs, outside and half a mile down the garden in an icy blast.

Maybe that was the moment the new businessmen of indoor plumbing started advertising their wares as 'life savers'.

SHROPSHIRE PRIVIES

Like little monuments they stand:
Some are cherished, more are not,
Some are humble, some are grand;
Just a few have got the lot.

In days gone by when folk would put
Their bums down in a little hut
To do what people had to do,
They'd hear the neighbours going, too.

Imagine! Getting out of bed
With one intent to start the day,
Eye firmly fixed on garden shed,
A shed, wherein true comfort lay.

Hoorah! For those that still remain
And in this book will live again
Each one special, each a star –
The Privies of Salopia

[9]

PRIVY DAYS AND PRIVY WAYS

> Clunton and Clunbury,
> Clungunford and Clun,
> Are the quietest places
> Under the sun.

So wrote A.E. Housman in his most famous verses – *A Shropshire Lad*. Housman (actually a Worcestershire lad who was potty about Shropshire) died in 1936. But if he returned today to those idyllic villages and hamlets around south Shropshire's Clun, he would still find them pretty quiet.

He would also discover that some of the same old facilities he'd have known are still there.

I'd arranged to meet Meryl Evans at the garage where she works, on the edge of Clun village. We were to retrace her steps, go back to her country childhood for the morning.

Today, privies were our topic.

Meryl and her sister Mary Ellis, who farms in Clun, were both brought up in the Old Farmhouse in the hamlet of Woodside, now an away-from-it-all B&B run by old colonials Margaret and Bob Wall, there for nearly 17 years.

But before we ever left the garage forecourt, Meryl told me that her boss, Grant Edwards, also had an outside job at his home, Ale Oak Grange about five winding miles away. Grant suggested I pop up then and snap his privy. 'Wendy's at home,' he said. He also agreed that Meryl could come with me before we continued to Woodside – and thank goodness for that.

Otherwise, despite being a Shropshire Lass (in my fashion

68

reporting days, that's what couturier Norman Hartnell used to call me, which dates me a bit) I might still have been wandering around the hills, lanes, tracks and moorland which make up this fabulous part of the world, flanked by Offa's Dyke and Clun Forest.

Ale Oak Grange was thought to be on a drovers' run in days gone by. No wonder landscape garden designer Wendy finds it an inspiring place to live and work. Apart from designing for others, she's also transformed chicken runs and rugged terrain into beautiful gardens. Wendy was a bit surprised, if amused, to see the potty loo woman asking to poke around the privy. She gently declined to pose with a pair of basic but effective wooden 'plugs' which would have fitted into the seat holes! The stone-built hut with its green, corrugated roof must boast one of the most entrancing views from any lavatory in Shropshire – and that's saying something.

Like so many more old thunderboxes, the loo with a view is used for storage now. But it was well worth the diversion.

And so to Woodside.

High above the cluster of Clun, the Old Farmhouse is a haven of holiday tranquillity for the modern-day traveller. Meryl and Mary remember it rather differently. The working farm kept all of them busy and memories are sharp of pigs hanging in the old kitchen, tin baths in front of the living room fire, the chap in Clun who had a marvellous garden and gave them the best rhubarb they'd ever tasted. Which was the clue to what I'd really gone to see. Because the old fellow's fruit was grown with that most common fertiliser – the contents of his privy.

Meryl and I drove over Clun's little stone bridge to collect Mary at the farm where she'd been on lambing night duty.

How excited the sisters were to see their stone-built privy still there over the sparkling and meandering little stream alongside the Woodside house. Not so sparkling in times past, though.

69

Sisters Meryl Evans (left) and Mary Ellis take a trip down Memory Lane to the privy of their childhood at Woodside, Clun.

Because the two-seater loo, used and scrubbed linen-white by several generations, was strategically placed above the water and its contents washed away downstream. Except, that is, in the sort of hard frosts Meryl and Mary say we've not had for this past 20 years.

As we took coffee with our hosts Bob and Margaret, Mary said expressively: 'The ice would be solid and everything from the lav would mount up on top of it. For some reason everybody always used the hole on the left, but when the stream froze and there wasn't any water, we'd use the other hole as well. Then when the thaw came everything would be washed away.'

Which reminded sister Meryl that their dad – a fortnight old when he moved to the house, he'd have been 101 on the day we gathered round his privy – then flooded the lower meadow with the . . . well . . . interesting stream water.

Bob Wall intends to restore this little slice of ablution history, which is around 150 years old.

The childhood memories were still being aired as we wended our way back down the hill to the village. Mary pressed half a dozen of her free-range eggs on me – so famous that one lady sends her son all the way from Swansea in South Wales to buy them.

It had been quite a morning in one of 'the quietest places under the sun.'

When I first started researching *Shropshire Privies*, apart from the funny looks, I got a host of people rushing to tell me unrelated snippets they seemed to have plucked from nowhere – just the odd closet comment or flash of memory collected over the years and waiting for some strange body like me to happen along.

Like the chap who said he'd heard that people in cottages at Darby Road, near where I live in Coalbrookdale, used to have to pop down the garden ... across the road. Yes, their facilities were for some reason separated from their houses by a strip of very public tarmac. I hadn't found anyone or any information to verify this until I asked the oracle of the Dale, Betty Duddell. She knew.

The former schoolteacher, 80 this year, has lived in her house on Coalbrookdale's Paradise since 1929 (oh yes, the road with a view is called Paradise and we in God's Own Valley have heard all the jokes!) close to the childhood home of legendary foot-baller Billy Wright. Her dad, Sid, was the caretaker of the old Coalbrookdale High School and her mum was the cook. As a former student, all these years on, I can vouchsafe that Mrs Duddell's Doorstep was just the job. That I now also live in the Dale is a real reward for some good I never knew I'd done. Betty has been here all the time and not a lot has passed her by.

As soon as I mentioned the Darby Road mystery, she said: 'Ah! I know about that. Mr Prince's mother told me it was due to the Squires family who lived at Strethill House. Mr Squires was at the Coalbrookdale works and it was his idea to re-route the road which then circled the works, so that it came between the houses and the toilets.'

The facilities were already tucked under the viaduct. So people lost their gardens and had to cross the road to get to the closets. 'They were not very happy, there were a lot of grumblings going on. But who do you think was the very first person to use that new road? Mr Squires himself when he was being taken to his funeral at the Quaker burial ground,' Betty clasped her hands together with glee.

Just to keep you on top of things, we *think* Mr Prince, who had the well-informed mother, was once at the local museum. And the ghosts of inconvenienced Darby Road residents past *know* that the grand finale journey of Mr Squires was poetic justice!

Betty's own lavatorial memories largely centre around the old cottages in The Forge at Coalbrookdale and Fountain Villa where her grandparents lived. Again, conveniently placed over a stream – the remains of which still criss-cross the road from upper Coalbrookdale to Dale End and into the River Severn – then the main highway for privy products to be dispatched into the river. 'The cottages didn't need the muck cart, you see,' Betty says cheerfully.

I came away from Paradise with enough tales for another book, a bunch of red camellias and an order never to give up on a camellia bush even if you think it's not going to flower. Seven or eight years later, it will undoubtedly burst into bloom. If Betty says so, it surely will!

I've known Alice Rickus for most of my adult life. She is a real east Shropshire character. Alice and her husband Jack lived in Spring Village, Horsehay, from where she ran the local Conservative branch and campaigned valiantly for the then Wrekin MP Captain Bill Yates (known as Domino Bill on account of playing the game in pubs throughout the area). The charismatic politician emigrated to Australia, became the first MP to sit in both the British and Australian parliaments and has since been governor of Christmas Island. He and his wife Camilla are still well, living near Melbourne and have stayed with us at Coalbrookdale on their visits to the UK. Alice has followed his every move.

She is 94 now, in a local home for old people, but her memory for those glory days of the 1960s is intact. Eyes sparkling, she remembers how she stood alongside Captain Bill in his opentopped Land Rover on his victory drives. She recited me her Bill Yates poem and recalled in detail Wrekin trips to London and beyond, organised by the Conservatives and ending up pretty well being led by Alice.

Her daughter thought she'd have some wonderful memories about privy days and privy ways. But apart from acknowledging the outside job 'with two holes in one' at the family home at Newdale near Lawley which nine of them (including seven children) had used, and the fact that she'd had one at her house in Horsehay, we didn't get much farther on privies. But forgive me if I indulge for a moment and record that, as a nipper, Alice had to scrub the stairs from top to bottom each Friday when she got home from school nearly 90 years ago. That the Christmas tree for the family was just a bough taken from a hedge. That a vicar of Lawley died in her arms (she used to work at the vicarage). And that she was the local lady who laid out. 'The police used to fetch me when anybody died. They'd say "fetch Alice". I'm very fond of laying people out.'

Why, I enquired gently. 'I don't really know, I just am.' Back to basics, she remembered: 'You were asking about the old earth closets weren't you? All I can say is that we had water put in ours at Spring Village, and we were very pleased to get it as well,' she nodded very firmly indeed. Final word. Lid down. Subject closed. God bless you, Alice!

74

[1 0]

THE POTTERS

Pop up and see me sometime, I still use an old earth privy, the message said. In days of clinical chain pulling and flushing, of instant, unseen disposal, feelings might be mixed about such an invitation. But to (by then) a seasoned privy investigator, the information was like manna. 'I've got one I still use'. . . magic.

The caller was potter (no jokes please) Elspeth Lamplugh who founded Willey Pottery down a track on the Willey Estate just outside Broseley. It's an idyllic spot and when Elspeth first arrived in Shropshire she rented nearby Jubilee Cottage from Lord Forester. That was in 1984. There was no electricity, one cold water tap in the scullery and the usual basic loo at the bottom of the sloping garden. Eventually the wash house became a little bathroom, lighting was still courtesy of Tilley or paraffin lamps and candles, and lavatory arrangements were as before. Though Elspeth confesses that on dark and cold nights a chamber pot filled the bill.

And doesn't romance work in curious ways? Because it was such an object which brought Elspeth and her husband Razz together.

At their first meeting, after hearing of her potty situation, Razz didn't rush out and buy her a bunch of red roses as consolation, he loaned her a commode. 'I don't know how he got it but it was a very nice one. And until you use both, you don't realise how much more comfortable a commode is than a chamber pot,' Elspeth said.

The rest, as they say, is history. The potter and the maths teacher got married and carried on living in tiny Jubilee Cottage for a while. But a baby – Sam was born nine years ago – allied

75

Elspeth Lamplugh – user. And proud as anything of her privy.

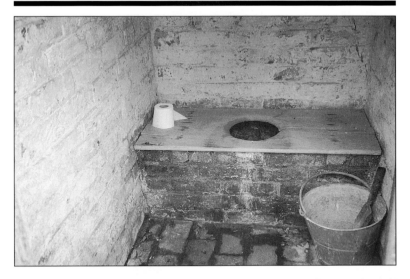

Pristine toilet roll, brush and bucket all give the game away. This one is used!

with a sudden desire for more space and things which switched on, saw them moving into nearby Broseley.

Now someone else is in the cottage, but Elspeth still works under her maiden name of Elspeth Soper at the bottom of the garden in the studio she had built in her time there.

There is still no electricity to her workshop so she makes her upmarket pots – sold in Ludlow and Much Wenlock galleries as well as farther afield in nice places like Hereford and Montgomery – with help of a leisure battery. 'I always wanted to make "pottery for the people",' she says, 'but you simply can't compete with Woolworths. So I make more individual pieces now. It's an expensive way to earn a living but having a husband who's a full time teacher makes it possible.' And, of course, Elspeth still uses her little earth closet when she's at work. A modern-day toilet roll on the seat is testament to current use.

Min Bland's Cardington privy has another on the neighbour's side.

78

'I love all that. I love sitting there and just thinking,' she says.

When the efficient, brick-lined pit is full, they simply shovel out the residue and dump it on the compost heap. 'I think you're meant to leave human compost for about two years before using it,' Elspeth adds as an afterthought. 'But then we put it on the garden.'

Quite!

It was a delightful chance that I should find a second potter with a privy. Min Bland and her late husband, who was a painter, were from the south of England and took on a cottage in the village of Cardington in the 1980s. They fell in love with it and Min loves it still, so stayed there after Bill's death.

We spent ten minutes (supervised by Min's devoted lurcher dogs) at the old 'facility' down the cottage garden with its one-hole seat generally adorned by a jug full of bamboo canes, and a whole Saturday afternoon tracing her extraordinary life. Apart from teaching pottery and being an expert on much of its history, she was also once a child model for a nun who was an artist. And so it was that Min came to feature on Christmas cards and paintings for the famous Medici company who specialise in those plump, angelic children.

The privy trail leads the investigator down many fascinating paths, not all of them to the loo!

[1 1]

THE GOSH FACTOR

When I was with the *Shropshire Star* newspaper, one editor, a Welshman called Bob Jones who still lives in the county, used to talk about the 'gosh factor'. If a picture or a story was so blessed, it meant that readers would be prompted to say 'gosh, fancy that' when they saw or read it.

You need the gosh factor in newspapers. And there is a rich seam of it in privy stories. I've certainly found plenty in Shropshire, not to mention the earthy language which peppers so many tales. Language which historians assure us was more normal and less shocking several generations ago.

Take Annie Bufton of Beveley in Telford, for instance. She's not greatly into privies herself – she collects stories about death as a hobby. But Annie treasures one family tale about a notorious relative. Her great-uncle (her mother's uncle) was the feared Enos Hoare who built rows of cottages in Oakengates and Old Park. Annie moved with her family into a rented Beveley cottage in 1974 when she was eleven. She finally bought it in 1996 and when she was looking through the deeds was amazed to find that the frightful Enos had built that one as well.

'He was as mean as anything. He'd save up all the string and match ends. And he'd walk for miles with his little leather bag to collect his rents,' she says. When his tenants couldn't pay, Enos would threaten to set fire to their outside lavvies like this: 'If the rent's not paid by Friday I'll burn the shit house down.'

Going home from the pub, fuelled with drink and bravado, locals used to sing their reply: 'Please don't burn our shit house down, mother will pay the rent. Please don't beat up father, the money's all been spent . . .' Annie can't remember the rest!

Concrete ruled in Ditton Priors, OK?

But she does know that Enos, a fiendish 5ft 1in tall, would fight with anybody. Well into his 80s, he could walk about quite safely with a wad of money – nobody dared mug or rob him. Interestingly, he apparently struck up a close friendship with a vicar of Wrockwardine Wood who became a partner in various projects, they even discussed opening a pub together! Enos died around 1943 at the age of 96 or 97.

Incidentally, although he never married, Enos Hoare was also very fond of the ladies ... and thereby, I'm told, hangs another way of paying the rent!

Even just visiting the privy wasn't always safe. Sylvia Stubbs from Ellesemere told me about her mum and dad (Walter and Daisy Roden) visiting aunt and uncle Bert and Dorothy

The listed urinal at Minsterley.

Norgrove at Rowton Farm on Lord Forester's estate. Walter was given a candle to light his way to the three-seater outdoor privy. Unfortunately, he threw the match into one of the holes. Flame met methane gas and ... whoosh! Walter went back to the house intact – but with the remains of his trousers in his hand.

What they were made of is also fascinating to the privy historian and it's not always brick or wood. For instance, rural Ditton Priors in South Shropshire once had a thriving concrete industry. Over the years, there have been some unlikely examples of concrete buildings in the pretty village, including lavatories. The outside loos at the popular Howard Arms pub and restaurant have functional and modern innards inside a good old concrete structure.

While tucked away on a corner in the village of Minsterley is that rarest of species – a listed loo in cast iron. This one is a men's urinal with a smart British Racing Green finish to its ornate panelling but offering just the same relief for the desperate.

Talking of Minsterley, in a rural valley not far away, Hollywood arrived in 1949 when camera crews came here to make *Gone to Earth*. The film of the famous novel by Shropshire author Mary Webb starred leading actress Jennifer Jones, Cyril Cusak and a young George Cole making his big screen debut.

Filming out in the sticks was a long and tedious process and locals still remember the great Miss Jones doing a deal with the occupants of a nearby cottage, the Gwilliam brothers, to use their earth closet. She availed herself several times a day and

Friends Mike and Sheila believe their plant pots are old Doulton loos.

left a whole half-a-crown on the side of the seat on each occasion. The brothers were very sorry to see her leave!

Friends Mike and Sheila have a pair of ornate pots – long since used for plants – which have been in their garden for more than 40 years. They have always believed that the pots with carved design in some sort of brown glazed pottery were old loos. They are so heavy, they've never been moved but each has a flat base with holes clearly once used to secure them. On close investigation, this privy hunter found the word 'Doulton' and 'patent number 17863'.

Royal Doulton couldn't immediately identify them. But curator Julie McKeown was intrigued and says that from the shape, the pots could well have been their water closets. The company certainly produced them in similar designs with the same sort of floor fixing, but while she found some in their old catalogues, there was nothing quite the same shape. So far, the Patent Office have been unable to to find a patent but they told Julie the pots would have been after 1887. Now everybody's interested and investigations continue . . .

Meanwhile, hilarious tales of what happened when townies met rural privies include the visiting suitor who was a bit posher than a lot. He was persuaded by his embarrassed girlfriend that the family lav was actually the basic but nevertheless sit-up and beg ceramic job with a flush system, just outside the back door of the adjoining house, rather than the earth closet behind their own property. The obliging neighbours romantically agreed to this deception, as a favour. Mr Posh never queried the unlikely trek and seemingly suspected nothing amiss as he was led through the front garden, down the footpath, alongside next-door's house and into their loo. Lovesick or what? It's not known whether that pair ever actually made it to the altar.

And one saucy tale made a memorable impact on Audrey Williamson from Much Wenlock. She remembers postman Eddie Wright telling her about his wife's family home at Shifnal where there was the familiar pigsty adjacent to the down-the-garden closet. An aunt, a city lass from Cardiff, arrived on a visit and her first trip to the privy was one nobody ever forgot.

Audrey chuckles: 'The family suddenly saw her running back up the garden with her knickers round her ankles screaming "Harriet, Harriet, help! The pig's had me arse." '

Even allowing for the minor poetic licence of someone running with their knickers round their ANKLES, the moment became memorable.

Janet Evans of Newport had told me about the two cottages out in the sticks which belonged to her family and where her dad once lived. Naturally they had outsiders, the contents of which were spread in the celery trench – they boasted the biggest sticks of celery around.

Local students now live in one of the dear little cottages in Outwoods and there is a typical brick-built privy on the edge of the adjacent field. If they're not in, just go and take a picture anyway, said Janet. So on a warm, idyllic Saturday morning, I did.

I climbed over the secure farm gate to be instantly surrounded by a flock of marauding sheep (well, four placid ones actually) who nudged, nestled and tried to eat my camera case. Undaunted, I got my picture and climbed back, over the gate ... at the feet of Maureen Hayes walking briskly down the lane with her collie dog.

Winifred Venables, unflustered by the appearance of a mad privy-searcher, poses outside her Outwoods privy.

Absolutely charming – and found by accident. Part of the stone complex at Damson Cottage.

Before they rounded me up, I felt bound to explain to Maureen what I was doing. She, in turn, told me she was coming to feed her sheep which grazed the cottage land. 'But if you're looking for privies,' she said, 'there's one at our house over there,' waving her arm out across the distant fields, 'and the other half of it is next door in mother's garden.'

So it was in my Shropshire meanderings, that I found the best complex of yesteryear. In solid grey stone, the block has a privy and a pigsty on each side and a bakehouse on the garden side of Maureen's mum, Winifred Venables.

After photographing at Maureen's place, I stood on the stool clearly kept for the purpose, and hailed Mrs Venables as she hung out the washing. To her eternal credit, she didn't bat an eyelid when this woman, over-excited about lavatories, accosted her across the fence. She simply invited me round, told me that she'd lived in the village for 57 years and had moved to the cottages when her husband died, they had previously been at the farm down the lane. She posed for a picture by her own privy and explained that son-in-law Bob was going to move the coal out of the bakehouse to tidy everything up. What a gem!

AND WHO COULD BLAME HIM!

Down in the south Shropshire village of Stottesdon, local odd job man Nipper Cook was asked by the vicar if he would empty the over-full earth closet for him. Nipper agreed but said it would be a day's work and the cost would be 10 shillings (or thereabouts). The deal was done and, on the appointed day, Nipper set to work with a vengeance. He did so well that he'd finished by lunchtime.

Off he went to the vicar, fully expecting his ten bob if not congratulations. But the reverend gentleman didn't quite see it that way.

'You've only worked half a day so you only get half the money,' he said, handing over just five shillings.

Locals swear that, during the night, an incensed Nipper went out, loaded up half the original contents . . . and dumped his load back in the vicar's closet.

The clerical response is not on record. But Nipper's photograph does hang proudly in the village's local pub, the Fighting Cocks.

[1 2]

RELIEF BY ANY OLD NAME

No matter what they called it,
However strange the name
When you paid a privy visit,
The relief was just the same.

Strange how names have varied so much when describing the trip to perform these necessary and mundane functions.

Coy euphemisms ranged from Down-the-garden, Up-the-alley, Thunder box, Rose Cottage and The Lav to House on the Thames (if they happened to be strategically over water, as many were), Number 10 (tut-tut to the old Shropshire lad who said that was a perfect name), Down Yonder and Up the Shut. While Outside Parlour, Popping to the Johnny, Visiting the Necessary, the bluntly descriptive Shithus and mysteriously 'I'm just going in the back yard' (not literally, we hope) were all used to explain a short but regular absence.

In later years Rocket Launch became in vogue and I heard Colin Young from Radio Shropshire refer to old privies simply as a plank of wood with a hole in 'em. You really can't argue with that.

But almost every name rooted in the past is so much more interesting and robust than those excruciatingly twee invitations passed on today to visit 'the little girls' room' or 'the little boys' place'. They didn't have crocheted toilet roll holders then, either.

As we now know, the nail on the wall to hold the squares of newspaper is all that was needed in the way of such artefacts. And when you had to balance a flickering candle or a torch

90

John Ferrington kindly sent me this record of a privy at New Works, near Little Wenlock.

91

with a dicky battery at the same time, functional rather than finery was the word.

This is how Peter Davies's *Mares Milk and Wild Honey, A Shropshire Boyhood* so charmingly describes the family's lavatory, Caroline by name: 'The little yard was big enough to enclose the pump, two or three chicken coops, bantam runs, a pig boiler, a coal hole, two pear trees, a damson tree and Caroline.

'Caroline was where you went after breakfast to make sure you would be all right for the day. You went there again before dusk to make sure you would be all right for the night.

'She (Caroline) was whitewashed, scented with Jeyes and very confidential. You knew if someone was coming down the path by the crunch of the cinders underfoot. We never locked the lavatory or any other door. Torn squares of *Home Notes* gave you all the help you needed if your boy had gone off with another girl. What you did if it was the other way round, you never found out. It did not give advice to boys whose girls had served them with that trick.'

But Caroline doubtless offered all creature comfort to the spurned. Spending a penny is a much more modern and less charismatic description of seeking relief – born after public conveniences started charging clients an old penny to go about their business.

If you've visited your American relatives, you'll be familiar with the Outhouse. While that other trans-Atlantic expression Comfort Station, which has crept into our vocabulary, is perhaps a bit nearer to the visits of yesteryear.

Because, leaving aside the night time terrors of darkness, spiders and rats, shutting yourself away in the privy is still remembered by many as a very comfortable experience. Birds twittering outside, a lilac bough over your head, a leisurely pipe of tobacco and a chance to catch up on the news you'd missed – even if it was only on small squares of paper so you never knew the end. With a precautionary foot wedged in the space below the door just in case anybody did think of barging in and, as a last resort, a well rehearsed whistle, the scene was set for many a quiet and contemplative moment.

I heard lots of variations of that story and even if distance lends enchantment to the view, it's a nice memory to have of life before the water closet.

Talking of which, the following tale tickled the fancy of several who sent it to me in various forms – all telling the same little story. This was Lynda Gardner's version.

An English lady was looking for a room for when she returned to live in Switzerland and asked the schoolmaster to help. They found one but when she went home to make final arrangements, she realised that she'd not spotted a lavatory, a WC. So she wrote asking the schoolmaster to check this out.

He had never heard the initials and, with help from the parish priest, decided that WC must mean Wayside Chapel (the alternative version of the cheeky tale refers to the local vicar and what he saw as an enquiry about a Wesleyan Chapel of which Shropshire has known many).

In this case, the schoolmaster sent off the following letter:

Dear Madam,

The WC is nine miles from the house in the centre of a beautiful grove of pine trees surrounded by lovely grounds. It will hold 229 people and is open on Sundays and Thursdays only.

As there are a great number of people expected in the summer months, I would especially recommend that you come early, although there is plenty of standing room. This is an unfortunate situation if you are in the habit of going regularly.

You will be glad to hear that a good number of people bring their own lunch and make a day of it while others who can afford a car arrive just in time. I would recommend you go on

Thursdays when there will be an organ accompaniment. The acoustics are excellent and the most delicate sounds can be heard everywhere.

It may interest you to know that my daughter was married in the WC. It was there that she met her husband. I can remember the rush there was for seats. There were two people in seats normally occupied by one. It was wonderful to see the expression on their faces .

The newest attraction is a bell which rings every time someone enters. And a bazaar is to be held to provide plush seats for all.

My wife is rather delicate so she can't attend regularly. It is almost a year since she went. Naturally, it pains her very much not to be able to go more often.

I shall be delighted to reserve the best seat for you where you will be seen by all.

Hoping to be of some service.

Schoolmaster.

As for that three-letter-word which so peppers the language, when did loo ever become . . . well . . . loo?

The Shorter Oxford Dictionary offers this hint:

1. A round card game. In three-card loo, the cards have the same value as in whist. In five-card loo, Jack of clubs is the highest card. A player who fails to take a trick or breaks the laws of the game is looed – required to pay a sum or 'loo' to the pool.

2. A velvet mask partly covering the face, formerly worn by women to protect the complexion.

3. To urge on with shouts.

4. A cry to incite a dog to the chase.

5. A loob (are we getting closer?), a pit or vessel into which the dross or earth is delivered by the trough; slime containing ore.

However, I go for the more likely derivation of the warning cry as the contents of the chamber pot were chucked into the street. Gardy loo, they'd shout merrily – a twist on the French expression 'gardez l'eau' (watch for the water).

And as for privy itself, the topic we've had such fun exploring in Shropshire's very own book, the choice may be private circle or companionship while Privy Chamber is 'a private room in which one is not liable to interruption or disturbance' – something you could hardly say about the lavatory arrangements of yesteryear.

Cheerio for now. Bottoms up.

ACKNOWLEDGEMENTS

To list here all the enthusiasts who helped would involve another book. So will all who are mentioned in *Shropshire Privies*, and those who aren't but offered information and memories, please accept my grateful thanks. I couldn't have done it without you. A word, too, for all whose privy tales didn't make it this time – thank you anyway.

Special appreciation to:

Sally Day for encouragement and many hours spent proof reading for me.

Holly, Daisy and Sam who sniffed around a few privies in our quest for the best.

Betty Duddell, the oracle of the Dale.

Rita Rich (as was) in Australia who linked me with Shropshire privies by e-mail.

Ludlow Castle ladies who put themselves out no end to help me find the long-drop.

Barbara and Barrie Trinder for their special interest.

Wolverhampton Express & Star – my own newspaper – for constant support.

For other invaluable publicity and encouragement: *Radio Shropshire, Shropshire Star, Telford Journal, Shrewsbury Chronicle, Shropshire Magazine*.

And absolutely everyone who helped make *Shropshire Privies* a reality, especially Suzanne and Nicholas Battle of Countryside Books who inspired and convinced me that privies are perfectly priceless.